PHILIPPIANS

LECTIO DIVINA FOR YOUTH

ANCIENT FAITH SERIES

Barefoot Ministries®
Kansas City, Missouri

Copyright © 2008 by Barefoot Ministries®

ISBN 978-0-8341-5021-8

Written by Tim Green
Editor: Mike Wonch
Contributing Editor: Bo Cassell
Assistant Editors: Robyn M. Lowery and Jeremy Coleson
Cover Design: JR Caines
Interior Design: Sharon Page

Adapted from *Lectio Divina Bible Studies: Listening for God Through Philippians*.

Green, Tim. *Lectio Divina Bible Studies: Listening for God Through Philippians*. Indianapolis, IN: Wesleyan Publishing House and Beacon Hill Press of Kansas City, 2005.

Library of Congress Cataloging-in-Publication Data

Green, Timothy Mark, 1961-
  Listening for God through Philippians / written by Tim Green.
    p. cm. — (Ancient faith series)
  ISBN 978-0-8341-5021-8
  1. Bible. N.T. Philippians—Devotional literature. 2. Bible. N.T. Philippians—Textbooks.
3. Youth—Religious life. I. Title.

  BS2705.54.G74 2008
  227'.600712—dc22

                                                                    2007036250

10 9 8 7 6 5 4 3 2 1

ABOUT THE
LECTIO DIVINA
BIBLE STUDIES

Lectio divina (pronounced lek-tsee-oh dih-vee-nuh), is a Latin phrase that means *sacred reading*. It is the ancient Christian practice of communicating with God through the reading and study of Scripture. Throughout history, great Christian leaders have used and adapted this ancient method of interpreting Scripture.

The idea behind *lectio divina* is to look at a Bible passage in such a way that Bible study becomes less about study and more about listening. The approach is designed to focus our attention on what God is saying to us through the Word. Through the process of *lectio divina* we not only read to understand with our minds, but we read to hear with our hearts and obey. It is a way of listening to God through His Word.

Some throughout history have said that *lectio divina* turns Bible study on its head—normally we read the Bible, but in *lectio divina*, *the Bible reads us*. That is probably a good way to describe it. It is God using His Word in a conversation with us to read into our lives and speak to our hearts.

In this series, we will use the traditional *lectio divina* model. We have expanded each component so that it can be used by both individuals and by groups. Each session in this study includes the following elements. (Latin words and their pronunciation are noted in parentheses.)

- **Reading** (*Lectio* "lek-tsee-oh"). We begin with a time of quieting ourselves prior to reading. Then we take a slow, careful reading of a passage of Scripture. We focus our minds on the central theme of the passage. When helpful, we read out loud or read the same passage over and over several times.
- **Meditation** (*Meditatio* "medi-tah-tsee-oh"). Next, we explore the meaning of the Bible passage. Here we dig deep to try to un-

derstand all of what God might be saying to us. We think on the passage. We explore the images, and pay attention to the emotions and feelings that the passage provides. We put ourselves in the story. We look for particular words or phrases that leap off the page as the Spirit begins to speak to us through the Word.

- **Prayer** (*Oratio* "or-ah-tsee-oh"). As we meditate on the passage, we respond to God by communicating with Him. We specifically ask God to speak to us through His Word. We begin to dialog with Him about what we have read. We express praise, thanksgiving, confession, or agreement to God. And we listen. We wait before Him in silence, allowing God the chance to speak.

- **Contemplation** (*Contemplatio* "con-tehm-plah-tsee-oh"). At this point in our conversation through the Word, we come to a place where we rest in the presence of God. Our study is now about receiving what He has said to us. Imagine two old friends who have just talked at length—and now without words, they just sit together and enjoy each other's presence. Having spent time listening to God, we know a little better how God is shaping the direction of our lives. Here there is a yielding of oneself to God's will. We resolve to act on the message of Scripture.

GROUP STUDY

This book is designed to be useful for both individual and group study. To use this in a group, you may take one of several approaches:

- **Individual Study/Group Review**. Make sure each member of the group has a copy of the book. Have them read through one section during the week. (They will work through the same passage or portions of it each day that week.) Then, when you meet together, review what thoughts, notes, and insights the members of the group experienced in their individual study. Use the group questions at the end of the section as a guide.

- **Group Lectio**. Make sure each member of the group has a copy of the book. Have them read through one section during the week in individual study. When you meet together as a group, you will study the passage together through a reading form similar to lectio divina:

- ○ **First, read the passage out loud several times to the group.** Group members respond by waiting in silence and letting God speak.
- ○ **Second, have the passage read aloud again to the group once or twice more.** Use different group members for different voices, and have them read slowly. Group members listen for a word or two that speaks to them, and share it with the group. Break into smaller groups if appropriate.
- ○ **Third, read the passage out loud again, and have the group pray together to ask God what He might be saying to each person, and to the group as a whole.** Go around and share what each person is learning from this process. At this point, review together the group questions at the end of the section.[1]
- • **Lectio Divina Steps for Groups.** Make sure each member has a copy of the book. As a group, move through the study together, going through each of the parts: reading, mediation, prayer, and contemplation. Be sure to use the group questions at the end of the section.

The important thing about using *lectio divina* in a group is to remember that this is to be incarnational ("in the flesh")—in other words, we begin to live out the Word in our community. We carry God's Word in us, (in the flesh, or incarnate in us) and we carry that Word into our group to be lived out among them.

The *Lectio Divina Bible Studies* invite readers to slow down, read Scripture, meditate upon it, and prayerfully respond to God's Word.

---

1. Parts of the "Group Lectio" section adapted from Tony Jones, *The Sacred Way: Spiritual Practices for Everyday Life*, Grand Rapids: Zondervan, 2005, p. 54.

CONTENTS

INTRODUCTION

Among the epistles included in the New Testament canon, Paul's letter to the Philippian church is seen as the most kind and gentle. It is very different from the strong reflection of Galatians or the deep theological lessons of Romans—the Book of Philippians is filled with rejoicing, prayerful thanksgiving, and loving compassion.

The city of Philippi was a successful Roman colony with citizens of Greek, Roman and Jewish backgrounds. The people were afforded the highly respected benefit of Roman citizenship. According to Luke's account in Acts 16:13-15, the church at Philippi was founded by the apostle Paul on his second missionary journey, and its first converts were Lydia and members of her household. Paul's compassionate prayer for the Philippian believers demonstrates his personal attachment to this family of faith (Phil. 1:3-11).

A dominant theme in this four-chapter book is that both Jesus Christ, and living the way He tells us to, have a direct impact on everyday life.

Paul wrote this letter from prison. This fact makes Philippians 4:6-7 all the more powerful: "Do not be anxious about anything, but in everything, by prayer and petition, with thanksgiving, present your requests to God. And the peace of God, which transcends all understanding, will guard your hearts and your minds in Christ Jesus."

NEVER ALONE IN THE JOURNEY
LISTENING FOR GOD THROUGH
PHILIPPIANS 1:1-11

SUMMARY

We are never alone in our walk with God. Although there may be times when we feel alone or discouraged, we share these experiences with our Christian family. There were several instances during the apostle Paul's ministry where he would have had the right to feel alone in his walk with Christ —times when he was locked in prison or under house arrest.

However, Paul was diligent and reported in his letters that he had many partners supporting him. Some prayed for him, some provided clothes and shoes and others helped with his workload. Paul knew that he belonged to a team, even when he was facing difficult situations. He knew he was being encouraged and supported.

Like Paul, we are part of a great team. Our lives are connected with fellow believers. Think about the close relationships you have with others in your youth group, or the feeling you get when hanging out with friends. Together, we share memories of yesterday and hopes for tomorrow, testify to great victories, and share the heavy loads.

PREPARATION ✟ Focus Your Thoughts

Who have been the two or three most influential people in your life? In what ways have these people influenced you? In what ways have they been partners or teammates in your life?

Think about ways that you have influenced others around you.

READING ✟ Hear the Word

The church at Philippi was one of Paul's great joys. It's no coincidence that the word *joy*, in some way, occurs 16 times in this letter. In Acts 16 we read of Paul's formation of this church. At Philippi, Lydia opened her heart to the Lord, and Paul and Silas experienced their miraculous escape from prison as they sang praises to God.

The friendly relationship between Paul and the church at Philippi continued for years. When the Philippians heard of Paul's imprisonment, they sent him a gift. In this letter, Paul expressed his thanks, not only for the gift, but also for the givers themselves.

Instead of including a traditional prayer of thanksgiving, Paul began this letter by describing his recent prayers for the Philippians as prayers of joy. Then he prayed for his Philippian partners, in particular, that their love would continue to mature.

Paul used several important words and phrases to express his prayer for the Philippians:

Partnership: Active participation.

Day of Christ Jesus: The return of Christ—when the work begun by Christ will be completed.

Fruit of righteousness: Concrete expressions of a right relationship with God.

Read Philippians 1:1-11, paying special attention to how these words and phrases shape the content of Paul's opening message to these beloved people.

MEDITATION ✿ ENGAGE THE WORD

Meditate on Philippians 1:1-8

Paul showed his gratitude for the Philippians, through his prayers that were filled with joy because of their partnership in the gospel. What do you think Paul means by *partnership?* What makes a relationship between people a partnership?

What other words might be used to describe this kind of relationship?

Read the quote by Dietrich Bonhoeffer. How is participating in a community different than simply belonging to a community?

> Christian brotherhood is not an ideal which we must realize; it is rather a reality created by God in Christ in which we may participate.
>
> —Dietrich Bonhoeffer, Life Together

Why would thinking about his partnership with the Philippians bring joy to Paul? What is joy? When have you experienced joy in your own life? Given the fact that Paul was in prison while writing this letter, what other circumstances in his life might have accounted for his ability to feel joy at that moment?

Can the Christian life be lived alone? Why, or why not?

Read the quote on page 15 by Kent Ira Groff. Do you agree with this statement? Why, or why not?

Without the discipline of community, solitude degenerates into self-absorption and isolation.

—Kent Ira Groff, Journeyman

Do you share a partnership with a fellow believer in Christ? What are the qualities of that relationship? Are your partnerships with other Christians important to you? Why, or why not? Compare the way you feel about your relationships with other Christians to the way Paul felt about his partnership with the Philippians. What could strengthen your partnership with other believers?

Meditate on Philippians 1:9-11

Since Paul had already acknowledged the love of the Philippians, why would he pray that their love would grow "more and more in knowledge and depth of insight"?

Compare the difference between the love Paul describes here and the sentimental emotions that our culture portrays as love.

Read the quote on page 16 by Carlo Carretto. What do you think about Carretto's statement concerning love?

> *Love will make demands on us. It will question us from*
> *within. It will disturb us. Sadden us. Play havoc with our*
> *feelings. Harass us. Reveal our superficialities. But at*
> *last it will bring us to the light.*
>
> —*Carlo Carretto, Why, O Lord?*

How does Paul's prayer here compare to his prayer in Colossians 1:9-12?

What do you think Paul means by the phrase *pure and blameless?* What misconceptions do you have about the term *pure and blameless?*

What is an example of a "fruit of righteousness"?

In what areas of your life are you seeking for God's guidance and direction in order to determine what is best?

Does your life show that you're completely loyal to Christ? What areas are hard to give to Christ?

What are the greatest challenges you face when it comes to bearing the fruit of righteousness?

PRAYER ✠ ASK AND LISTEN

Seek the face of God. Ask, "Lord what are You saying to us today?"

Pray that God will help you find others with whom you may partner with on the journey of faith. Join with one other person to pray the prayer of Charles Wesley. Ask God to make you a dependable partner.

> Help us to help each other, Lord,
> Each other's cross to bear;
> Let all their friendly aid afford,
> And feel each other's care.
> —Charles Wesley, "Jesus, United by Thy Grace"

CONTEMPLATION ✠ REFLECT AND YIELD

Think about your relationship with God. Have you tried to walk with God by yourself?

What are ways that you can connect and form a partnership with other Christians?

What are ways you can be a positive influence on the Christian life of another? How can you allow other Christians to be a positive influence on your Christian life?

GROUP STUDY

- Do you think it's easy for Christians to feel like they have to walk with God on their own? Why, or why not?

- Do you think that our culture contributes to our self-sufficient attitude, even when it comes to our faith?

- Are there areas in your life where you feel no one can help you?

- What is the benefit of a partnership with other believers?

- What are ways you can form a partnership with other believers?

- Why is being "filled with the fruit of righteousness" important in our relationship with God and living the Christian life?

- Read over any particular scripture that was important to you, and discuss as a group how it is significant to your own life.

TRIUMPH THROUGH ADVERSITY
LISTENING FOR GOD THROUGH
PHILIPPIANS 1:12-30

SUMMARY

Bad things happen to everyone—even good people. So the question is not whether we will encounter difficulties, but how will we react when bad things happen to us?

Paul's life is a testimony of our ability to grow in adverse situations. In 2 Corinthians 11:23-28, Paul recited a long list of trials he had faced. Yet, he did not waste time wondering why tough times had come. He simply acknowledged that they were there. In spite of the difficulties he had faced, Paul remained confident and faithful. He never gave up, but continued to run the race of faith. He was convinced that whatever the situation, God could transform it into a triumph.

This should be no surprise to followers of Jesus Christ. At the core of our faith is the belief that Jesus died for our sins and rose again. No matter what dark situation you find yourself in, Jesus always provides the light.

As a follower of the resurrected Christ, you can discover victory in Him.

PREPARATION ✝ FOCUS YOUR THOUGHTS

Describe a time when you experienced hardship. How did you respond to that situation? Was it easy to keep in mind you are never alone, and Jesus is always by your side?

List some reactions you've had when seeing people suffer during difficult times. How have you helped friends in your youth group, or at school, overcome hard times?

READING ✝ HEAR THE WORD

At the time of his writing to the Philippians, Paul was imprisoned, most likely under house arrest in Rome (see Acts 28:14-31).

The congregation at Philippi was also facing trials of their own. While we are not certain of their specific struggles, we know that some were being persecuted by civil officials. In addition, some teachers who were preaching a message different than that of Paul were entering the church. This may have led to internal struggles (see Phil. 3:2, 18-19; 4:2). When writing to the Philippians, Paul used his own suffering as an example for dealing with the difficulties they were facing. But

Paul didn't make himself out to be a hero. He pointed to the success of the gospel that had resulted from his suffering.

In his encouragement to the people at Philippi, Paul used the following terms:

Palace guard: This term may refer either to a governor's palace in a Roman province or to a group of several thousand soldiers in Rome.

Chains: While Paul may literally have been in chains, the term is a metaphor for his suffering, specifically his imprisonment.

Exalted in my body: The term *exalted* or *lifted up* reminds the readers of Christ being lifted up on the Cross.

Live your lives: Literally, *live as citizens,* thus a reminder of their true citizenship.

Contending as one man: Working together as a team.

Read Philippians 1:12-30.

MEDITATION ✝ ENGAGE THE WORD

Meditate on Philippians 1:12-14

Paul told the Philippians that the harsh conditions he encountered, specifically his imprisonment, had served to promote the gospel. Read the quote by Carlo Carretto. What does this statement say about the work of God's kingdom?

> This is the truth. The will of God is fulfilled in spite of us ... and even with us sometimes.
>
> —Carlo Carretto, Why, O Lord?

Paul saw his adversity as a witness to those who were causing his suffering as well as to others in the prison. How was Paul a witness to these people?

What is there about Paul's adversity that would have pointed to Christ?

Read the quote by Hermann Bezzel. How do Christians most often deal with suffering? Why would Bezzel say that "suffering is the greatest work in the discipleship of Jesus"?

> Suffering is the highest action of Christian obedience; and I call blessed, not those who have worked, but all who have suffered. Suffering is the greatest work in the discipleship of Jesus.
>
> —Hermann Bezzel, quoted in Pastoralblatter

How would Paul's adversity have encouraged fellow Christians to speak the Word of God more courageously?

Have there been times where you've seen your friends, or adult leaders turn a negative situation into a positive one? What effect did this have on you? Did you find yourself being encouraged to overcome difficulties in your own life?

Are "chains" for Christ something we decide to take up on our own, or do they come to us? Explain your response.

What "chains" for Christ are you wearing right now?

Meditate on Philippians 1:15-18

What do you think Paul meant when he said that some preach Christ out of envy, rivalry, and selfish ambition? Have you ever listened to a sermon, or been a part of a small group where the speaker/leader seemed to be involved for selfish reasons? Have you seen someone share the gospel and make it more about them and less about God? How did that make you feel, and how did you respond?

Does Paul's response to people who preach the gospel for false motives surprise you? Why, or why not?

What has Paul's attitude taught you about conflict among God's people? Have you experienced conflict between friends, or even youth group members? How was your attitude in comparison to Paul's?

Read the quote by Stephen V. Doughty. In what ways can conflict among the people of God actually lead to growth?

> The more I see of conflict in the church, the more I am moved by persons who allow conflict to become the occasion of their growth. . . . Jesus seeks to form us even in the places of greatest friction. In the midst of division and hurt, He can draw us toward maturity in fresh and formative ways.
> —Stephen V. Doughty, Discovering Community

How do you handle conflict among God's people? How does our culture (movies, television, video games, etc.) teach us to handle conflict? Do the views of our culture differ from the views that Paul preaches?

Do you find it difficult to accept Paul's idea that the most important thing is that Christ is preached, regardless of the motives of those involved? Why, or why not?

Meditate on Philippians 1:19-26

Paul was confident that no matter what happened to him, Christ would be exalted in his body. What do you think he meant? Do you feel like you live a life where no matter what happened to you, Christ would be exalted?

Read the quote by Simone Weil. Do you agree with this statement? Why, or why not?

> *Affliction makes God appear to be absent for a time, more absent than a dead man, more absent than light in the utter darkness of a cell. A kind of horror submerges the whole soul.*
>
> —*Simone Weil, Waiting for God*

How can we praise Christ through suffering and death?

Do you believe that Paul wanted to continue living and preaching the gospel, or to die and be with Christ? Explain your response.

Could you honestly make the statement that Paul made: "For to me, to live is Christ and to die is gain"? If not, what changes in your thinking would need to occur before you could make such a statement?

Meditate on Philippians 1:27-30

What does a life look like that is "worthy of the gospel of Christ"? Does your life look like this? What are areas in your life that you need to give over to God?

Paraphrase what you think Paul meant by saying, "You stand firm in one spirit, contending as one man for the faith of the gospel."

Has there been an instance where your youth group faced a difficult experience, and you all had to "stand firm in one spirit"? What was the outcome of that situation?

Read the quote by Dom Augustin Guillerand. How do you normally respond when you find faults in your life? Do you feel the need to be perfect? How do you get past your own weaknesses?

> *God will know how to draw glory even from our faults. Not to be downcast after committing a fault is one of the marks of true sanctity.*
>
> —Dom Augustin Guillerand

Do you prefer to work out difficult situations on your own or with the help of others? Why?

PRAYER ✠ ASK AND LISTEN

Seek the face of God. Ask, "Lord, what are You saying to us today?"

In silent prayer, submit your adversities to God and ask, "Lord, how can You be glorified in this situation?" Ask God to meet your greatest need, no matter how big or small.

CONTEMPLATION ✠ REFLECT AND YIELD

How would your life change if you adopted Paul's attitude that "to live is Christ and to die is gain"? If everyone in your youth group decided to make this change, how would it affect the group dynamic?

What would change in your life if you lived every moment in "a manner worthy of the gospel of Christ"? Think of what would happen if every believer changed his or her life in this way.

GROUP STUDY

- What is the hardest part of remaining positive during a time of adversity?

- Discuss the ways we can overcome the trials in our lives. How does God help us during these trials?

- What part of this chapter hit home the most? What was it about that part that was so easy to relate to?

- Do you ask God, "Lord, how can You be glorified in this situation?" whenever there are difficult times in your life? What is your first reaction when you are faced with a difficult circumstance?

- What are ways that your youth group can encourage each other during difficult times?

- On a 3"x5" index card, write down two things you could do the next time you encounter adversity. (This might include prayer, reading the Bible, and talking to a Christian friend.) Keep this card close and pull it out any time you face a difficult situation.

A NEW WAY OF THINKING
LISTENING FOR GOD THROUGH
PHILIPPIANS 2:1-18

SUMMARY

Living the Christian life is more than changing old habits. It's more than a transformation of lifestyle (Rom. 12:1-2). Ultimately, it is our minds that are changed after we come to Christ.

Paul invited the Philippian believers to begin thinking like Jesus Christ, which would involve a spiritual death and resurrection.

This would have been difficult in the self-centered, accomplishment-driven society in which the Philippians lived. This new way of thinking would call for a lifestyle in which all actions were considered with the interest of other people in mind.

Although the Philippian church was a generous congregation, this challenge would have seemed impossible. However, Paul's call for them was not just to try harder to be good but to be transformed into the likeness of Christ through the power of the Holy Spirit.

Like the Philippians, you, too, are surrounded by a self-centered, accomplishment-driven culture. And, like them, God calls you to participate in this alternative way of thinking—to take on the mind of Jesus Christ.

PREPARATION ☦ FOCUS YOUR THOUGHTS

Describe a time when someone tried to change your mind. Think about your school elections. What did the student running for president do to try to persuade or change you? What methods do you use to try to change the minds of others?

Did it work? Did your thinking really change, or did you continue in your old way of thinking?

READING ☦ HEAR THE WORD

Paul told the Philippians to live together in unity. While we have no indication that there were significant conflicts in that congregation, Paul did request assistance in helping two women, Euodia and Syntyche, to "be of the same mind in the Lord" (Phil. 4:2, KJV). Paul called the Philippians both *communally* and *individually* to participate in the mind of Jesus Christ. In what may have been an early hymn describing Christ's suffering, death, resurrection, and ascension, Paul sets the standard for the Christian worldview. It is the mind of Christ (2:6-11).

Read Philippians 2:1-18, paying particular attention to these key terms in Paul's admonition:

Like-minded: Having one mind—the mind of Christ.

Something to be grasped: Grasped can mean "to hold on to." It can also mean "to exploit" or "to take advantage of."

Made himself nothing: Literally, this phrase means "He emptied himself."

Nature: This word, which can also mean *form*, describes the manner in which Christ was actually God, but took on the form of a servant.

Work out your salvation: This phrase does not imply that we are saved by what we do, but that we should act upon what we believe.

Drink offering: An Old Testament ritual expressing gratitude.

MEDITATION ✟ ENGAGE THE WORD

Meditate on Philippians 2:1-5

Throughout his letter Paul spoke of the joy the Philippian church gave him. What could it mean that they would make his joy complete?

Describe what your youth group would look like if it were

"like-minded, having the same love, being one in spirit and purpose." If your youth group was like-minded, would anyone be allowed to disagree?

Is there a difference between *uniformity* and *unity*? If so, what is it? To which did Paul call the Philippian Christians?

What would your youth group look like if it did nothing out of selfish ambition, but acted in concern for others? What prevents you and your peers from doing this? What prevents congregations from doing this?

In what areas of your life do you observe selfish ambition or pride?

In what specific relationships in your life is God calling you to look to the interests of others? Do you find that difficult to do? If so, why?

Meditate on Philippians 2:6-11

What do you think Paul meant when he said that Jesus made himself "nothing"?

What incidents in the life of Jesus illustrate this self-concept?

Where in Jesus' life might He have been tempted to abandon the role of servant?

Read the quote by Henri Nouwen, Donald McNeill, and Douglas Morrison. Do you agree with the statement? How does this idea compare to your understanding of the nature of God?

> [Jesus'] becoming a servant is not an exception to His being God. His self-emptying and humiliation are not a step away from His true nature. His becoming as we are and dying on a cross is not a temporary interruption of His own divine existence. Rather, in the emptied and humbled Christ we encounter God, we see who God really is, we come to know His true divinity.
>
> —Henri Nouwen, Donald McNeill, and Douglas Morrison, Compassion

What difference does it make that the adoration of Christ is based upon His humiliation through suffering and death?

What attitudes or opinions that you hold would need to be changed if you were to take on the role of servant? When you think of the term "servant," what is the first thing that comes to mind?

If you were to take on the role of servant, how would that affect your relationships?

It has been said that there is no resurrection without crucifixion. If you were to embrace that concept, how would it affect your life?

Meditate on Philippians 2:12-18

As a strong believer in God's grace, Paul certainly did not promote the idea that we are saved by works—that is, because of the good things we do. Yet, he knew that the mind-set of Christ must be applied to day-to-day living.

Read the quote by Teresa of Avila. In her opinion, what is the relationship between belief and action?

> Our works have no value unless they are united with faith, and our faith has no value unless it is united with works.   —Teresa of Avila, Interior Castle

Because of Paul's caution to work out our salvation with fear and trembling, what is the significance of his next statement: "It is God who works in you to will and to act according to his good purpose"?

How would you describe the relationship between *willing* and *acting*?

How will you work out the mind of Christ in your school or part-time job? your home? your youth group?

Read the second quote by Henri Nouwen. Describe the cross you are presently carrying.

> *Each of us has a cross to carry. There is no need to make one or look for one. The cross we have is hard enough for us! But are we willing to take it up, to accept it as our cross?*
>   —*Henri Nouwen*, Bread for the Journey

How does it affect your walk with God to know that He enables you to both will and act for His good purposes?

PRAYER ✞ ASK AND LISTEN

Seek the face of God. Ask, "Lord, what are You saying to us today?"

Open your mind to God, asking Him to transform your mind to be like the mind of Jesus Christ.

CONTEMPLATION ✞ REFLECT AND YIELD

How would the most important relationship in your life change if you were to think the way Christ thinks?

What mind-sets or attitudes would you like to see transformed by God's grace?

GROUP STUDY

- Discuss three relationships in which your behavior will be affected by adopting the mind of Christ.

- What are some ways that you can practice placing the interests of others ahead of your own selfish wants and desires?

- In what ways do you put yourself before others?

- What is the hardest part about putting others before yourself?

- How do you think the world's perception of Christians would change if every believer had the attitude of putting others first?

- What are qualities of a Christ-like mind that you would like to see developed in yourself?

- What part of the scripture reading spoke to you the most?

- What do you think God is saying to you? How will it impact the way you live this week?

LITTLE PEOPLE, GREAT TASKS
LISTENING FOR GOD THROUGH
PHILIPPIANS 2:19-30

SUMMARY

The Bible is full of many heroes. We look up to great people, such as Sarah and Abraham, Miriam and Moses, Deborah and Gideon, Mary and Peter. There are several others who have done important things, but they are easily forgotten. These lesser-known heroes also carried out great tasks for the Kingdom. However, they are more often placed in footnotes than on pedestals. Where would the kingdom of God be without this mass of unspoken heroes who have been faithful in the little things?

Paul often refers to the unknown Kingdom builders throughout his letters. He knew that faithful followers of Christ—who don't seek fame—are very important. Centuries later, the kingdom of God is still advanced by women and men who are simply willing to be available whenever and wherever the Lord calls.

Are you?

PREPARATION ☦ FOCUS YOUR THOUGHTS

Think about the Kingdom builders from the Bible who didn't receive widespread recognition, but did significant work for God. Name three people who are not widely known, but have had a significant impact on your life.

What did these people do that profoundly affected you?

In one word, describe the character of each person.

READING ☦ HEAR THE WORD

Paul used this letter to describe his plans to send Timothy and Epaphroditus to Philippi. Although Paul did not completely abandon the subject under discussion, his description of both men builds nicely around the topic which centered on the mind of Christ.

In the introduction to Philippians, Timothy is described as the co-sender of the letter. Timothy had accompanied Paul and Silas on their second missionary journey (see Acts 16), where Paul had established the church at Philippi. Timothy's visit would be a return to the church he had helped found.

Epaphroditus brought gifts, from the church at Philippi, to Paul in prison. Epaphroditus had become seriously ill. Although he had recovered, the people back in Philippi had become worried about his illness. Paul had determined to send Epaphroditus back home with this letter in hand.

Read aloud Philippians 2:19-30.

MEDITATION ✝ ENGAGE THE WORD

Meditate on Philippians 2:19-24

Reflect on the difference between Paul's comment that Timothy took "a genuine interest" in the Philippians' welfare and his comment that "everyone looks out for his own interests and not those of Jesus Christ." Compare these statements to Philippians 2:4.

Why would he say he had no one else like Timothy?

Describe Timothy's character. How frequently do you encounter people like Timothy? Would you consider your character like that of Timothy's?

Read the quote by James C. Fenhagen. Why is compassion such a rare occurrence in our society? Do you agree with Fenhagen that the loss of compassion threatens human survival?

> It might well be that the greatest threat to human survival now confronting us is not the loss of energy or the increase of pollution, but the loss of compassion.
> —James C. Fenhagen, Mutual Ministry

Do you know someone who demonstrates the same attitude that Timothy had? Describe that person. What types of characteristics do they portray?

Is Paul right in saying that most people look out for their own interests? Do you find yourself wrapped up in your own wants and needs? What causes some people to be more concerned with others than with themselves? What characteristics do they possess?

Read the quote by Sadhu Sundar Singh. List a few reasons why we don't reach out in selfless concern to other people.

> We ought to make the best possible use of God-given opportunities and should not waste our precious time by neglect or carelessness. Many people say: there is plenty of time to do this or that; don't worry. But they do not realize that if they do not make good use of this short time, the habit formed now will be so ingrained that ... this habit will become our second nature and we shall waste that time also.
> —*Sadhu Sundar Singh*, With and Without Christ

Describe a time where you found it difficult to take an interest in the welfare of someone else.

Are there people in your life that are easy to care about? Who are they, and what makes it easier to take an interest in them? Do those same people find it easy to care and take interest in you?

Are there people in your life that are difficult to care about? Who are they, and what makes it so difficult to care about them? What types of characteristics describe those people?

Meditate on Philippians 2:25-30

Paul describes Epaphroditus as his brother, fellow worker, and fellow soldier. What does each of these descriptions say about Epaphroditus's relationship to Paul? Is there a relationship in your life that compares to that of Paul and Epaphroditus?

How does Epaphroditus's willingness to risk his own life relate to the challenge Paul gave the Philippians in 2:3?

Is there anyone in your life that you might call brother or sister—someone who will stand by you and fight battles with you? Could you say these things about a fellow youth group member, or possibly a school friend?

Do you know anyone whose life reflects the character traits of Epaphroditus? In what ways has that person been willing to take risks or sacrifice for others?

In which situations might you be willing to be an Epaphroditus?

In which situations would you find it difficult to be an Epaphroditus?

Read the poem by Teresa of Avila. Do you believe what she says? Why, or why not?

Christ has
No body now on earth but yours;
No hands but yours;
No feet but yours;
Yours are the eyes
Through which He looks
Compassion on the world;
Yours are the feet
With which He is to go about
Doing good;
Yours are the hands
With which He is to bless now.

—Teresa of Avila

PRAYER ☩ ASK AND LISTEN

Seek the face of God. Ask, "Lord, what are You saying to us today?"

Join with a prayer partner and offer yourselves to God. Ask Him to show you ways to be a servant to others. Ask Him to take away the selfish thoughts that cloud your mind. Then allow Him to speak to you.

CONTEMPLATION ✟ REFLECT AND YIELD

What obstacles prevent you from being a servant to other people?

How might you overcome those obstacles?

Are you ready to offer your life in service to other people if God were to open a door for you?

GROUP STUDY

- How would you describe someone who has a "servant's heart"?

- In what ways are you serving others?

- In what ways might God be calling you to serve others?

- Discuss a time when another person put your needs above their own. How did that make you feel?

- What was the most challenging part of this section?

- What have you learned from the biblical text that was studied, and how will you let it impact your life?

- Think of one person you will encounter this week to whom you might be of service. What will you do to serve him or her?

MORE THAN PERFORMANCE
LISTENING FOR GOD THROUGH
PHILIPPIANS 3:1-11

SUMMARY

A performance-driven mind-set dominates our culture. We often believe that "if it is to be, it is up to me." This thinking can affect the way we think about our relationship with God. It can be tempting to believe that it is the good things we do that advance our standing in God's eyes.

Our culture isn't the only one to suffer from this problem. Paul confronted this way of thinking throughout his ministry. Various religious teachers influenced the congregations Paul had established and preached a gospel other than that based on grace. Galatia is an example of this type of occurrence. In his letter to the Galatians, Paul exclaimed, "You foolish Galatians! Are you as foolish? After beginning with the Spirit, are you now trying to attain your goal by human effort?" (Gal. 3:1, 3).

From the earliest days of Christianity, the human desire to earn God's acceptance through religious or moral achievements has been a serious problem. Just as Paul challenged the earliest Christians to trust in the saving work of Christ alone, God calls us to a wholehearted reliance upon His grace. He calls us to move beyond a religion based on performance to a relationship based on faith.

PREPARATION ✦ FOCUS YOUR THOUGHTS

In what areas of your life do you feel driven to perform or achieve?

Have you ever felt like the depth of your relationship with Christ depended on how many "spiritual acts" you completed?

READING ✦ HEAR THE WORD

In his letter to the Philippians, Paul takes a different path with the introduction of the word *finally*. About halfway through, Paul moves beyond his discussion of the partnership among Christians and having the mind of Christ to focus on one of his deepest, most heartfelt convictions about salvation: that it is a relationship with Christ resulting from grace alone. In this passage Paul corrects the misunderstanding of some of the Philippians.

Apparently, the Philippian church had been hearing the

teachings of a certain group of Christians demanding that non-Jewish believers be circumcised. In Paul's mind, the rite of circumcision—required by law for Jews—represented an action that some might take with the motive of attempting to gain God's favor. Paul became upset for that very reason. He firmly believed that "if righteousness could be gained through the law, Christ died for nothing" (Gal. 2:21). In his discussion, Paul makes reference to several significant terms:

Dogs: A metaphor describing the destructive nature of the people teaching works-based salvation.

Mutilators of the flesh: People demanding the circumcision of others.

Confidence in the flesh: Trust in human resources or achievements.

Know: More than knowledge of facts, intimate participation in a relationship.

Righteousness: A right relationship with God and with others.

Read aloud Philippians 3:1-11.

MEDITATION ✟ ENGAGE THE WORD

Meditate on Philippians 3:1-6

Paul begins this section of his letter by warning against those who teach that a relationship with Christ is grounded in human ability or actions. He doesn't take lightly the false messages the people were preaching and described them as *dogs* and *mutilators of the flesh.*

Why would Paul take this matter so seriously? Why is this issue so important for Christian disciples to understand?

In referring to human performance in Philippians 3:4, Paul uses the word *flesh*. What are some other words that could be put in its place?

List the areas that Paul mentions from his religious past in which he might have placed his confidence. If Paul had been writing today, what kinds of achievements might he have named?

What areas of your own life have tended to make you feel self-confident about your relationship with God? Does being actively involved in your youth group, or Church, make you feel more confident in your relationship with Christ?

Why do you think it's easier for people to look at their achievements or performance as indicators of their own goodness, rather than relying only on God's grace?

Do you think it makes sense to rely on your own effort to make yourself a better person? Why, or why not?

Meditate on Philippians 3:7-9

Paul says that what was once in the profit column of his life is now in the loss column. What did he want the reader to gain from this message?

Paul said that every previous source of his confidence is now a loss in contrast to the "surpassing greatness of knowing Christ Jesus." How is knowing Christ more valuable than personal efforts or achievements?

Read the quote by Charles de Foucauld. What does this statement mean for people who place their confidence in their own resources?

> You give your help, not in proportion to our merit, but to our needs. You came for the sick and not for the healthy.
>
> —Charles de Foucauld, *Meditations of a Hermit*

Righteousness ultimately means having a right relationship with God and with others. Describe a relationship you have that is based on law. (A relationship based rules or guidelines. A coach might be an example.) Then describe your relationship with God—a relationship based on grace. Compare and contrast the two.

Which type of relationship do you think would be easier to maintain? Which would be more fulfilling? Explain your reasoning.

Read the testimony of John Wesley. In what ways does Wesley's testimony affirm Paul's teaching?

> About a quarter before nine, while he was describing the change which God works in the heart through faith in Christ, I felt my heart strangely warmed. I felt I did trust in Christ, Christ alone for salvation: And an assurance was given me, that He had taken away my sins, even mine, and saved me from the law of sin and death.
> —John Wesley

Is your relationship with God based on law or grace?

What items in your personal profit column need to be placed in the loss column?

Read the statement by Richard Rohr. Do you believe this? Why, or why not?

> Spirituality is about seeing. It's not about earning or achieving. It's about relationship rather than results or requirements. —Richard Rohr, Everything Belongs

Meditate on Philippians 3:10-11

Paul concluded this section of his letter by explaining what it means to know Christ. For Paul, this knowledge of Christ is an intimate partnership. Throughout his letter, Paul has spoken of partnerships; now he describes the details of a partnership with Jesus.

How would your life be different if you shared in Christ's sufferings and death?

How is knowing Christ and knowing *about* Christ different? How does really *knowing* Christ, on a relational level, impact your life?

Is your desire to know Christ driven by your head or by your heart? How would you like to see your knowledge of Christ grow, and what could you do to aide this growth?

In practical terms, what does it mean to suffer and die with Christ?

How might suffering and dying with Christ become just another way of trusting in our own abilities or achievements?

Read the quote from Gregory of Nyssa. What does it mean that we can share a friendship with God? How do you react to that idea?

> *Since the goal of the virtuous way of life is the very thing we have been seeking, it is time for you, noble friend, to be known by God and to become His friend.*
> —*Gregory of Nyssa, The Life of Moses*

PRAYER ✝ ASK AND LISTEN

Seek the face of God. Ask, "Lord, what are You saying to us today?"

Paul makes a clear distinction between performing religious acts and having a grace-based relationship. Which method of relating to God best describes your life? Pray silently, "I want to know You," then listen for God's direction.

CONTEMPLATION ✝ REFLECT AND YIELD

In the midst of your hurried, achievement-oriented schedule, stop! Become silent before God and reflect on His amazing grace. Now hear Him say to you, "My grace is sufficient."

Discuss a few ways that you can put your busy lifestyle on hold and take the time to develop your relationship with Christ— maintaining a grace-based relationship rather than law-based.

GROUP STUDY

- In what ways would your spiritual life be changed if you were to place everything you have done in the loss column of your life, and rely only on Christ for your sense of righteousness?

- In what ways would your relationship with God be transformed if you were to participate in Christ's suffering, death and resurrection?

- Name two areas of your life in which Christ is calling you to suffer, die and rise with Him.

- In what ways would your youth group be affected if everyone involved focused on having a friendship with Christ?

- How would developing your friendship with Christ help you be a witness to others?

- Name two actions you will take this week that will help you know Christ more fully. Then, create a plan that will enable you to follow through with those actions.

PRESSING ON AND STANDING FIRM
LISTENING FOR GOD THROUGH PHILIPPIANS 3:12—4:1

SUMMARY

In a world that craves fast food and instant gratification, we often hear the cry: "I want it! And I want it *now!*" It is easy to have the same way of thinking in regards to our spiritual life, and sometimes we look for a quick fix to spiritual problems. We want spiritual maturity, and we want it *now!*

One of the apostle's favorite metaphors for the Christian life was a race. Paul encouraged the Corinthians to "run in such a way as to get the prize" (1 Cor. 9:24). Near the end of his ministry, he announced that he had "fought the good fight" and "finished the race" (2 Tim. 4:7). For Paul and other early Christians, the Christian life was not a destination; it was a journey.

As a follower of Christ, you, too, are called to remain focused and to keep running the race—to remain faithful in your relationship with Christ.

PREPARATION ✠ FOCUS YOUR THOUGHTS

Have you ever run in or watched a race?

What characteristics have you seen in successful competitors?

What potential obstacles do runners face that could prevent them from finishing? How do they avoid or overcome them?

READING ✠ HEAR THE WORD

Paul talked about sharing in the suffering, death, and resurrection of Christ, and right after, describes the Christian life as a race. Paul didn't want the Philippians to think he was claiming to be perfect like Christ, so he quickly goes on to say that he had by no means reached the final destination. He then emphasized two important attitudes that a believer should have about the Christian life. First, because the "race" is yet unfinished, there is always room for growth—we should keep pressing on. Second, we should be careful not to slip back or lose ground in our spiritual journey. So the goal of the Christian life, Paul says, is to press on and stand firm.

To describe this, Paul uses several important terms throughout the text:

Perfect: In this context, *perfect* means completed or finished.

Forgetting: Counting as no value.

Prize . . . heavenward: Paul admits he has not experienced the ultimate transformation—resurrection—but he moves toward the goal.

Mature: This is the same word translated as *perfect* in verse 12. Here it describes those who were serious about making progress in the Christian life.

Read Philippians 3:12—4:1.

MEDITATION ⚜ ENGAGE THE WORD

Meditate on Philippians 3:12-14

Paul wanted it to be clear that he had not achieved all he described in the previous verses. He never wanted the people to be confused and think that he was finished with the race, and in essence, perfect. When he wrote that he had not obtained "all this," what do you think he was talking about?

Why do you think Paul was so determined to make this point?

Why do you think it was important to Paul that Jesus had first taken hold of him?

Paul said that he was forgetting what was behind. Do you think Paul was able to forget his past? Why, or why not?

Read the quote by Paul W. Chilcote. Can you relate to what he is describing? In what ways do you struggle with your past, and the person you were before Christ came into your life?

> What a strange thing to be new and old at the same time, to be recreated by your love and yet continue to struggle with my old self. You have freed me from the guilt and power of my own brokenness, but inner healing requires a long process of divine therapy.
> —Paul W. Chilcote, Praying in the Wesleyan Spirit

Paul talked about "pressing on" as straining toward what was ahead. What do you think Paul meant by "the prize"? Does this effort by Paul turn the Christian life into another performance-driven activity?

Read the statement by Mother Teresa. What do you believe she means by a "real living determination"? What does that type of determination look like?

> Our progress in holiness depends on God and ourselves—on God's grace and on our will to be holy. We must have a real living determination to reach holiness.
> —Mother Teresa, A Gift for God

What are the positives of seeing what is ahead for us in our spiritual lives? How can we guarantee that the statement, "I have not been made perfect," does not become an excuse for spiritual immaturity? Would this be an easy statement to make so you don't have to try as hard?

What is in your past that still needs to be forgotten? Why is it so hard for us to forget the past?

Could your present spiritual experience be characterized as "pressing on"? Why, or why not?

What obstacles lie between you and the goal of spiritual maturity?

Read the quote by John Wesley. In response to Paul's description of the Christian life as a race, what do you believe Wesley meant by "one design, one desire"?

> Always remember the essence of Christian holiness is simplicity and purity: one design, one desire: entire devotion to God.   —John Wesley

Meditate on Philippians 3:15—4:1

Paraphrase this statement: "Let us live up to what we have already obtained" (3:16).

What do you think the Philippians had already gained? What might have caused the Philippians to move backward?

Paul described certain people, saying, "Their destiny is destruction, their god is their stomach, and their glory is in their shame." What do you think their lives were probably like? How would you rephrase that verse so it makes more sense in our current culture?

Read Mark 8:33. How does this verse relate to Paul's statement, "Their mind is on earthly things, but our citizenship is in heaven"?

How does identifying oneself as a citizen of heaven promote "standing firm" on earth?

Specifically, what does it mean for you to live up to what you have already obtained? What does it mean to stand firm?

Read the quote by Joyce Rupp. Do you agree with her statement? Why, or why not?

> One of the dangers of spiritual growth is that too much emphasis can be placed on "results," on how we are doing or how we are progressing.
>
> —Joyce Rupp, The Cup of Our Life

What people or circumstances in your life are most likely to influence you to move backward? Are there situations that you have put yourself in that delay your spiritual journey?

Read the quote by Johann Arndt. Explain what you think Arndt means when he says that love of the world can conquer the soul and the spirit.

> The love of this world, pleasure, and pride is a strong sweet wine by which the soul and the spirit are conquered.   —Johann Arndt, True Christianity

Would you say that your life better reflects your citizenship on earth or in heaven? Why? Are you satisfied with your current lifestyle? What things, if any, would you change about the choices you have made in the last few months?

PRAYER ☩ ASK AND LISTEN

Seek the face of God. Ask, "Lord, what are You saying to us today?"

Allow God to speak wholeness into your life as you come silently before Him. Focus on these words of Jesus from John 14:27: "Peace I leave with you; my peace I give to you."

CONTEMPLATION  REFLECT AND YIELD

The Christian life doesn't consist of arriving at one spot and standing still. It is a journey. What is the next step you believe God is calling you to take on the journey to spiritual maturity? What will you do about that this week?

GROUP STUDY

- Do you feel that you are pressing on, standing still, or moving backward in your spiritual life?

- What things in your life does God invite you to forget?

- Are you ready to let go of the past and move forward?

- How does it make you feel to view your Christian life as "running the race"? Does this image help you understand what it means to persevere through the difficult times?

- Pray as a group, and ask God to reveal any area of your life where you need to stand firm or press on. What do you think God's direction is for you in those areas of your life?

- For the next two weeks, keep a paragraph journal of your Christian "race". Include the way God helps you press on in your faith journey. Find a partner or group who will join you in this exercise, so that you can share your experiences with each other.

CHRISTIAN LIVING IN THE REAL WORLD
LISTENING FOR GOD THROUGH
PHILIPPIANS 4:2-9

SUMMARY

Living a Christian life isn't like living in a dream world where everything goes smoothly. Rather, the Christian life includes everyday relationships, ordinary concerns, and the routine matters upon which we focus a good deal of our time and energy.

Although Paul focused on issues of belief, he ended his letters with simple, practical advice on applying faith to life. Paul also personalized greetings and addressed people by name, specifying the issues they were facing. Paul was in touch with where people were at in their everyday lives.

The gospel of Christ impacts everyday life. It affects relationships, daily choices, habits, and patterns of thought. God cares about your beliefs, but he is also concerned with the way you live out those beliefs in daily life.

PREPARATION ⚜ Focus Your Thoughts

If someone wrote a song about your life, what would the title be? Why?

List three words that describe your day-to-day life.

If you could change one thing about your life, what would it be?

READING ⚜ Hear the Word

At the conclusion of his letter, Paul encouraged the Philippians to live a life modeled after Christ. Up to this point, Paul focused on his partnership in the gospel with the Philippians and on their shared partnership in the suffering, death, and resurrection of Christ. At the end of the letter, Paul described in realistic terms what that partnership would look like.

Paul asked that Euodia and Syntyche (two women that weren't often mentioned) be of the same mind in the Lord. Basically, he wanted them to embody the mind of Christ that he had described earlier (Phil. 2). To urge this request upon the two women, Paul appeals to someone addressed as *syzygus*, which is translated *yokefellow*. Although this word may be a personal name, the term was probably chosen to emphasize the need for partnership among believers, Paul's major theme in this letter.

As you read Philippians 4:2-9, note how Paul describes the comprehensive nature of the Christian life.

Gentleness: Bearing with or giving consideration to other people.

Peace: Not an absence of turmoil but wholeness experienced in spite of turmoil.

Guard: A military term meaning to place a protector around.

MEDITATION ✟ ENGAGE THE WORD

Meditate on Philippians 4:2-3

Compare Paul's message in Philippians 2:5 to that of 4:2.

Why do you think Paul asked his "loyal yokefellow" to help in the matter involving these women? In what way do you think Paul expected this person to help?

Have you ever witnessed a conflict between two Christians? Name some reasons such conflicts occur.

Have you ever been a part of a conflict with another Christian? What was the root of that conflict? Compare a conflict that you've had with another Christian to a conflict you've had with a non-believer.

Read the quote by Hannah Whitall Smith. If we saw Christ in a person with whom we had a conflict with, how would it affect our attitude and actions?

> Nothing else but this seeing God in everything will make us loving and patient with those who annoy and trouble us. . . . Christians often feel at liberty to murmur against people, when they would not dare to murmur against God.   —Hannah Whitall Smith,
> The Christian's Secret of a Happy Life

Is conflict between Christians always wrong? In general, is conflict wrong? Why, or why not?

If both parties in a conflict had the "mind of Christ," what effect would that have on the conflict? Describe how both the attitudes and actions would be different.

Why do people often allow conflicts to persist without working toward resolution?

Meditate on Philippians 4:4-7

Paul's call to rejoice is linked to two significant cautions: to give consideration to others and to trust God. How do you believe these two factors relate to joy?

Is it easy for you to get impatient with others?

Do you think it is realistic of Paul to expect others to be completely free from worry?

Compare what Paul said here about anxiety to what Jesus said in the Sermon on the Mount (see Matt. 6:25).

From your point of view, what is the connection between prayer and worry?

What is the relationship, if there is one, between experiencing peace and being patient with others?

What is your attitude like when you're around a group of people? Are there certain people that cause you to get easily frustrated? Why do you find it harder to be patient with them?

Are there things going on in your life right now that are leading to worry and anxiety? In general, what types of things cause you to worry?

What do you do to relieve your anxiety or worry?

Read the quote by John Wesley. What would it mean to pray like a child?

> *Pray, just as you are led, without reasoning, in all simplicity. Be a little child, hanging on Him that loves you.*
>
> —John Wesley

Why is it important to express thanks to God when making requests of Him? Why do you think people so often fail to do that? When you do something nice for someone would you like a "thanks" in return?

Read the quote by Dietrich Bonhoeffer. What is your reaction to his statement?

> *Only he who gives thanks for little things receives the big things. We prevent God from giving us the great spiritual gifts He has in store for us, because we do not give thanks for daily gifts. . . . We pray for the big things and forget to give thanks for the ordinary, small (and yet really not small) gifts. How can God entrust great things to one who will not thankfully receive from Him the little things?*
>
> —Dietrich Bonhoeffer, Life Together

What are needs that you might bring to God? What are things that you are thankful for?

Meditate on Philippians 4:8-9

Paul's final words of wisdom explain what the Philippians should focus their attention on. Why is it important that Christians choose carefully what they think about?

Read the quote by Susannah Wesley, spoken to her children. Describe how this mother's advice relates to the various terms used by Paul in verse 8.

> Whatever weakens your reason, impairs the tenderness of your conscience, obscures your sense of God, or takes off the relish of spiritual things, whatever increases the authority of your body over mind, that thing for you is sin.   —Susannah Wesley

Examine the terms used in verse 8. Name something in your life that each term could describe.

Do you focus your attention regularly upon things like these? Why, or why not?

PRAYER ✞ ASK AND LISTEN

Seek the face of God. Ask, "Lord, what are You saying to us today?"

Paul urges his Christian friends to apply their faith to the everyday affairs of life. In silent prayer, ask God to guard your heart and mind with His peace.

CONTEMPLATION ✞ REFLECT AND YIELD

Name one person with whom you might demonstrate greater patience. Name one worrisome circumstance that you will submit to God in prayer.

GROUP STUDY

- How would your day-to-day life change if you were to demonstrate greater patience with troublesome people?

- How would you handle conflict differently if you saw Christ in everyone?

- Why do we choose to worry rather than present our concerns to God?

- How would your life change if you were to consistently present your requests to God?

- How would your life change if you were to think more intentionally about the things that become the focus of your attention?

- Determine this week to allow the gospel of Christ to affect your attitudes and relationships.

THE LIFE OF CONTENTMENT AND GRATITUDE
LISTENING FOR GOD THROUGH
PHILIPPIANS 4:10-23

SUMMARY

Do you ever think about the problems you're facing in life and wish things could be different? Sometimes it really is true that "the grass is always greener on the other side of the fence."

If there was a person who could have wished for his life to be different, it was the apostle Paul. Throughout his ministry, Paul faced persecution, imprisonment, rejection, and sickness. Even in the midst of hard times, Paul never seemed to indulge himself in the daydream of a carefree life. While not eager to experience problems, Paul was able to appreciate and celebrate the grace of God he experienced during hardship. By having this mindset, he was able to find both contentment and gratitude in spite of his difficult situation.

Like Paul, you can experience contentment as you express gratitude for God's faithful presence in your life no matter what circumstances you face.

PREPARATION ☦ FOCUS YOUR THOUGHTS

If you could change one thing about your life, what would it be?

If you could always keep one thing the same what would it be? Why?

READING ☦ HEAR THE WORD

At the conclusion of his letter, Paul acknowledged a gift sent by the Philippians. While we don't know much about the gift, we do know that this was not the first time they assisted the apostle. Throughout Paul's ministry the Philippians had been the most generous of all the churches. Paul even mentioned their generosity in one of his letters to Corinth (2 Cor. 8:1-5; 11:9).

Paul made it clear to the Philippians that he was not completely dependent upon their gifts. At the same time, he wanted them to know how much he appreciated them. He expressed contentment during his troubling circumstances and gratitude for all that they had done for him.

Paul used various phrases in expressing his gratitude:

To be in need: This is the same word used in 2:8 to express the idea that Christ "humbled" himself.

Credited to your account: Paul borrowed language from the

world of commerce to show that the Philippians had received dividends from the gift they had invested in Paul's ministry.

Fragrant offering: Related to Israelite offerings of thanksgiving to God.

Sacrifice: In 2:17, Paul referred to the sacrifice coming from the people's faith; their faithful gift is viewed as a sacrifice of thanksgiving.

Carefully read Philippians 4:10-23.

MEDITATION ☦ ENGAGE THE WORD

Meditate on Philippians 4:10-14

At the same time Paul thanked the Philippians for their gift, he explained that he would be okay even without their generosity. What events in Paul's life might have helped to teach him the lesson of contentment?

How would you define *contentment?* Is there a difference between contentment and happiness? Why, or why not? Are you content or happy with your life right now? Are you both?

Paul says he has learned the secret in being content in any and every situation. What do you believe this secret is?

Do you think it is possible to be content in all situations of life? Why, or why not?

What is the relation between Paul's statement that he can do all things through Christ, and the contentment he has discovered?

Compare what Paul wrote here with his words in 2 Corinthians 12:7-10. What similarities or differences do you see in these passages?

Name a circumstance or situation in your life that caused you to feel discontent. If Paul were to give you advice about that situation, what do you think he might say?

Read the quote by William Shakespeare. Does it help to remember God's past faithfulness when thinking about your current troubling situation?

> God's goodness hath been great to thee; Let never day or night unhallowed pass, But still remember what the Lord hath done. —Williams Shakespeare

Do you believe that you, too, can do all things through Him who gives you strength? Why, or why not?

Meditate on Philippians 4:15-23

Paul listed the times in which the Philippians had shared his problems. What do you think Paul meant by saying that they "shared" his troubles?

Why do you think the generous actions of the Philippians made such a profound impact upon Paul?

Read the quote from Henri Nouwen, Donald McNeill, and Douglas Morrison. Why is it easier to give gifts or money from a distance than to get close to people in need?

> It is not bending toward the underprivileged from a privileged position; it is not a reaching out from on high to those who are less fortunate below; it is not a gesture of sympathy or pity for those who fail to make it in the upward pull. On the contrary, compassion means going directly to those people and places where suffering is most acute and building a home there.
>
> —Henri Nouwen, Donald McNeill, Douglas Morrison,
> Compassion

What did Paul mean when he wrote that rather than looking for a gift, he was looking for what the Philippians had credited to their account by giving to him? In what ways does giving a gift benefit the giver?

Why do you think Paul called the service of the Philippians a pleasing sacrifice to God when it was Paul that they served? Read Micah 6:6-8 and compare that prophet's words with Paul's statements to the Philippians. In what ways are they similar? Are there any differences?

In verse 19 Paul suddenly shifted the focus away from himself, saying, "My God will meet all your needs." Why might Paul have made this shift?

What do you think Paul meant by "all your needs"? What things do you need? What things do you want but don't really need?

Read the words from the Shaker song. How does the call to simplicity help us understand the genuine needs of our lives? Is there a relationship between practicing simplicity and experiencing contentment? If so, what?

> 'Tis the gift to be simple, 'tis the gift to be free, 'tis the gift to come down where we ought to be, And when we find ourselves in the place just right, 'twill be in the valley of love and delight. — 18th-century Shaker Song

Describe a time when someone shared in your adversity or you shared in someone else's. What impact did this have on you? How did this impact your relationship with the other person?

Do you struggle to accept the idea that God will meet all of your needs "according to His glorious riches in Christ Jesus"? If so, why? What might make it easier for you to accept that belief?

PRAYER ✢ ASK AND LISTEN

Seek the face of God. Ask, "Lord, what are You saying to us today?"

Choose a prayer partner. As you pray together, ask God to make His strength real in your lives.

After praying, speak these words of affirmation to one another: "My God will meet all your needs according to His glorious riches in Christ."

CONTEMPLATION ✢ REFLECT AND YIELD

How would your life be different if you could learn to be content in every situation?

In what areas of your life do you most need the assurance that you can do all things through God's strength?

GROUP STUDY

- What types of situations are you facing right now that cause you to depend completely upon God's strength?

- Finish the sentence: The secret to experiencing contentment in my life this week is to . . .

- Do you think if you led a simple life, only fulfilling your true needs, that your life would be more content? How does our culture go against "simplistic" living?

- Is it hard for you to remember that God is always with you, especially throughout your most troubling times? Why do you think it's so hard to keep that in mind?

- Do you think having compassion for other people leads to more contentment within your own life? Why, or why not?

- More often than not, are you the person giving the gifts or receiving the gifts? How does it make you feel to give rather than receive?

- How has reading the Book of Philippians made a difference in your faith journey?